"Produced by special arrangement with
Original Works Publishing.
www.originalworksonline.com"

Cover photo by Antonio Miniño.
Amanda Jones as Anaïs Nin.

ANAÏS NIN GOES TO HELL
© David Stallings
Trade Edition, 2019
ISBN 978-1-63092-118-7

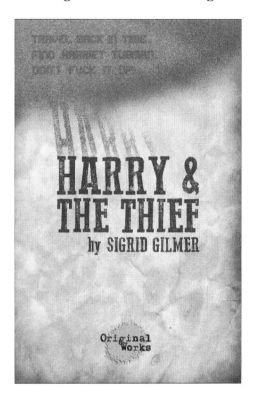

HARRY AND THE THIEF
by Sigrid Gilmer

Synopsis: Mimi's cousin Jeremy has a PhD in physics, a brand new time machine and a plan. He's sending Mimi, a professional thief, back to 1863 to change history by providing Harriet Tubman with modern day guns. Lots and lots of guns.

Cast Size: Diverse Cast of 10 Actors

ANAÏS NIN GOES TO HELL

A comedy of mythic proportions by
DAVID STALLINGS

ANAÏS NIN GOES TO HELL was first presented at the New York International Fringe Festival by Maieutic Theatre Works at the Connelly Theater in New York City, on August 8, 2008 under the direction of Cristina Alicea, with the following cast:

ANDROMEDA	Marnie Schulenburg
HELOISE	Aly Wirth
JOAN OF ARC	Colleen Piquette
CLEOPATRA	Maggie Benedict & Kristina Kohl
VICTORIA	Madalyn McKay
ANAÏS NIN	Shelly Feldman
BOSIE	Jeremy King

Producers, Julie Griffith & Antonio Miniño; set by Stephanie Tucci; costumes by David Withrow; lighting by Dan Gallagher; sound by Martha Goode; stage manager, Stuart Shefter; assistant stage manager, Jonathon Saia; Publicist, Katie Rosin of Kampfire PR.

ANAÏS NIN GOES TO HELL was first produced Off-Off Broadway by Manhattan Theatre Works at the Theater at the 14th Street Y in New York City, on October 14, 2016 under the direction of Antonio Miniño, with the following cast:

ANDROMEDA	Mlé Chester
HELOISE	Mel House
JOAN OF ARC	Stephanie Willing
CLEOPATRA	Nylda Mark
VICTORIA	Madalyn McKay
ANAÏS NIN	Amanda Jones
BOSIE	Richard Lindenfelzer
MARC ANTONY	James Edward Becton
OPHELIA/KAREN/FRIDA	Hannah Seusy

Producer, Martha Goode; set by Blair Mielnik; lighting by Dan Gallagher; costumes by Izzy Fields; sound by Martha Goode; line producer, Collin Bradley; stage manager, Rachel Denise April; assistant stage manager, London Griffith; assistant director, Natalie Marmol; Publicist, Katie Rosin of Kampfire PR.

CHARACTERS

ANDROMEDA
Greek princess of legend. She is in her early twenties, sweetly innocent–almost a child, but genuine.

HELOISE
Twelfth Century nun. She is in her thirties-forties and wears a severe nun's habit. She has a dark sense of humor.

JOAN OF ARC
She is an intense, tiny woman in her twenties-thirties with the haircut of a boy.

CLEOPATRA
Empress. She is a dark-skinned, and sultry woman in her thirties-forties who possesses a remarkable beauty paired with a sharp wit.

VICTORIA
Queen of England. She is a severe woman of late-middle age and large stature.

ANAÏS NIN
Writer, philosopher, analyst, and poet from the twentieth century. Anaïs comments on everything and knows nothing. She is in her thirties.

LORD ALFRED "BOSIE" DOUGLAS
Poet. Bosie is well dressed and delicately handsome, in his early twenties.

MARC ANTONY
Lover. Forties. Antony is a strong, hearty man with a forlorn nature.

OPHELIA/KAREN/FRIDA
A frail beauty with a delicate voice—at the end of the play a vibrant Frida Kahlo.

PRODUCTION NOTES

The Karen Carpenter songs in the play have lyrics intentionally altered, as Karen's journey has continued in the afterlife and she no longer sings the same stories. Similarly, the melodies should be varied and changed over time—not identical to the original but off balance and altered. In former productions there was no literal water. In the opening scene. For example, in one of the productions Andromeda tried to kill herself by putting a pillow over her face to cause suffocation. The Hydra has been accomplished through sound and lighting design, no need for a literal monster, simply imagination.

ANAÏS NIN GOES TO HELL

ACT ONE: *The Women Who Wait*

PROLOGUE

(Ophelia floats onstage, most of her body submerged. She seems a frozen vision.)

OPHELIA *(sung in Elizabethan style)*: They bore him
barefaced on the bier;
Hey non nonny, nonny hey nonny;
And in his grave rain'd many a tear
Hey nonny, nonny non

And will a' not come again?
And will a' not come again?
No, no he is dead:
Go to his death-bed:
He never will come again.

(Spoken) "To be or not to be", that was always
A question men by force answered for me.

(Sung) The water oh that day was clear;
Hey non nonny, nonny hey nonny;
My skin turned blue but not from fear
Hey nonny, nonny non

Oh what is it that she hides?
Oh what is it that she hides?
A child in her grows.
And no one must know.
This mother has not been a bride.

(*Spoken*) And so the queen, his mother watched me drown
And would not stop me for the precious crown
Would never to a bastard given be.

(Sung) You would not write my scene hey nonny nonny
Hey non nonny, nonny hey non
Remember me pristine hey nonny nonny
Not who I was. Not who I am.
The whole of me invisible through history.
Hey nonny nonny non.

(Spoken) There's Rosemary, that's for remembrance; pray you love, remember.

(The Hydra rises and eats Ophelia.)

SCENE 1:

(The play is set on an island surrounded by the river Styx. The stage should be surrounded by water, or lit so that the effect of reflected moonlight is seen on the faces of the actors. The sand is black, like volcanic ash. The play opens to midnight darkness. Karen Carpenter sings a twisted version of "Rainy Days and Mondays", softly from her own island, which we see from a distance. The silhouetted image of two women is seen, staring into the void of nothingness before them. Heloise is a twelfth century nun dressed in black with a tight wimple covering her head. She mouths the words of a Latin prayer and clutches an oversized rosary with oversized wooden beads. Beside her sits Andromeda, a Greek of tremendous beauty.)

KAREN *(sung)*: Singin' to myself and feelin' lost.
> Sometimes I'd like to leave
> But all I can do is grieve.
> Hangin' around, some kind of lonely clown
> Rainy eternal Mondays always/

HELOISE *(sung as a Gregorian Chant)*: Salve, Regina, mater misericordiae: vita, dulcedo, et spes nostra, salve… /Keep it down Karen.

(Karen stops.)

ANDROMEDA: I like that song/

HELOISE: Audite me, Asa et omnis Iuda et Beniamin! Dominus vobiscum, quia fuistis cum eo.

ANDROMEDA: Heloise. Please? I know you stopped praying decades ago—

10

HELOISE *(rocking intensely in prayer)*: Kyrie Eleison. Christe Eleison. Kyrie Eleison—

ANDROMEDA: I won't let it happen again, Heloise. No. It's not—*not* going to happen—

HELOISE: It is coming soon.

ANDROMEDA: No! It isn't. No. I'm not—*not* going to let you do it. No—

HELOISE *(urgently)*: It is coming!

ANDROMEDA: No. No-no-no.

HELOISE: I feel it!

ANDROMEDA: I don't care—I *don't* care! It doesn't come—It never comes—It never will come.

HELOISE: I'm disappointed in you, Andromeda. You sound like Sylvia.

ANDROMEDA *(darkly)*: Don't you dare…

HELOISE: It's been a while since the Hydra had a meal.

ANDROMEDA: I hate Sea Monsters.

HELOISE: Then, I wouldn't go around saying you don't think the men will come. I honestly have a feeling. Andromeda...they will.

ANDROMEDA *(with longing)*: But Heloise. They never do.

(A signal is heard off stage, the sound of a hollow conch shell being blown. Heloise falls to her knees and clutches her rosary.)

HELOISE: Pater oster qui es in coelis!

ANDROMEDA: I don't believe in monotheism!

HELOISE: The shell...it was the signal!

ANDROMEDA: I'm not—*not* falling for this again.

HELOISE: The luxury of genius is that there are so few of us, but that is also our misery... That was the shell—I can't fake the signal!

ANDROMEDA: She could be in on the joke.

HELOSIE: Joan of Arc doesn't make jokes…

(Andromeda strains harder to see.)

ANDROMEDA: I see nothing/

HELOSIE: /You heard the signal!/

ANDROMEDA: /Nothing—

HELOISE: A light! I see a light! I see it!

ANDROMEDA: Darkness—only darkness! My eyes are blinded by darkness!

(Heloise grabs Andromeda's face and points it at an angle.)

HELOISE: There! *I* see it! *You* see it! The signal sounded—*she* sees it!

(*Heloise lets go of Andromeda and waves her arms. Andromeda drops back to her knees and crawls to the water.*)

ANDROMEDA: I want to die.

HELOISE: Stop it. Stop it now. It's coming! I see a light!

ANDROMEDA: I want to die!

HELOISE: You're an idiot!

ANDROMEDA: I want to die! I want to die!

(*Andromeda puts her head under water in an attempt to drown herself. Heloise puts her foot on the back of Andromeda's head, Andromeda struggles under water.*)

HELOSIE: I'm fucking with her. It always fascinates me how people can force themselves to cling to a lie. It's easy for a idiot to believe in a small lie—but the more educated you are the more likely it is you believe in a big lie. A whopper. Because it's *taught* to you. And when you believe in a big lie—oh—you clutch it with all of your being even to destruction. It's drilled into you like a personal scripture written on the inside of your skin. I believed in a big lie. I believed in God and I believed with all my spirit and here I am. I haven't seen heaven or hell. I see nothing but this damned island and these damned women and you know what the kicker is? I am the only intelligent one. God has abandoned me with fools, so who can blame me if I fuck with them!

(Heloise releases her foot; Andromeda raises her head and gasps.)

ANDROMEDA: I—I—I was trying to kill myself.

HELOISE: I see a light!

ANDROMEDA: I was trying to end my life and you did nothing!

HELOISE: They'll be here soon!

ANDROMEDA: There is no boat!

HELOISE: You are near-sighted!

ANDROMEDA: But what if I could? What if I could die twice?

HELOISE: You can't. You've tried. Remember?

ANDROMEDA: No.

HELOISE: There was the time you threw yourself off a cliff/

ANDROMEDA: That was so scary—I thought I was going to die—

HELOISE: You didn't—you're dead. Oh! And there was the time you joined Joan of Arc in the re-enactment of *her* death—you got a little crispy.

ANDROMEDA: But what if I could die twice? Would you save me?

14

(Beat. Probably not.)

ANDROMEDA: I know I don't see well. Do you really see a light?

HELOISE: Yes. It's there. I swear.

ANDROMEDA: Heloise! What if—if—if—it's *him*? What if he's finally come!

(The conch shell calls again. Both women react, screaming with exuberance.)

HELOISE: Benedictus Comeatus Phallus Maxima!

ANDROMEDA: Benedictus Comeatus Phallus Maxima! Oh! If it's him will you be happy for me? If—if it's mine—if he comes? I'd be happy for you—if—

HELOISE: Yes!

ANDROMEDA: Do you really see a light!

HELOISE: Yes! Yes! Andromeda, yes!

(Andromeda gasps.)

ANDROMEDA: Oh my gods! I see it! I see it! I really see it!

HELOISE: Do you really!

ANDROMEDA: I do! I do! Oh Heloise, I see the light!

(They embrace.)

HELOISE: Where?

ANDROMEDA: What?

HELOISE: I want you to show me where you see it.

ANDROMEDA: Why? You see it too.

HELOISE: I want to make sure we're looking at the same thing.

(Andromeda points.)

ANDROMEDA: There—there it is.

HELOISE: You don't see the boat.

ANDROMEDA: What—what did I say?

HELOISE: That's not where it is.

ANDROMEDA: It is—I see it—

HELOISE: Fine.

ANDROMEDA: I see it!

HELOISE: Of course you do.

ANDROMEDA: You don't believe me?

HELOISE: No.

ANDROMEDA: By the gods I see it! I—I do! And it's—it's him—I *know* it's *him*!

HELOISE: There is no light.

(Beat.)

ANDROMEDA: You said there was…

HELOISE: There's no light.

ANDROMEDA: The alarm sounded twice.

HELOISE: It was false.

ANDROMEDA: But Joan of Arc doesn't lie.

HELOISE: I told her I had a vision from God and that she was supposed to sound the alarm whether she saw something or not. She'll do anything if you say it's a message from God.

ANDROMEDA: You lied—you—*lied* to me again. Why?

HELOISE: I have nothing else to do.

ANDROMEDA: It makes you laugh?

HELOISE: Yes.

ANDROMEDA: It makes you laugh to hurt me?

HELOISE: Yes.

ANDROMEDA: I want to go to sleep—I wish we could *sleep*.

(They have not slept for centuries. A small light begins to shine from off stage.)

HELOISE: So do I.

ANDROMEDA: Will they ever come?

(The light is getting brighter. Neither woman notices it.)

HELOISE: I used to believe they would. He would at least. Mine would come. And then I thought...no. And now I have no thoughts.

ANDROMEDA: You always have thoughts. I never do. Tell me a story.

HELOISE: You know everything about me.

ANDROMEDA: But I don't remember. Tell me about yours. Your man.

(Andromeda crawls to Heloise and puts her head on her lap. The light gets more intense, illuminating.)

HELOISE: He was a philosopher. He was a teacher. He was my lover.

ANDROMEDA: What was his name?

HELOISE: Abelard.

ANDROMEDA: Yes. And was he beautiful?

HELOISE: No. He was ugly. He thought I was beautiful.

ANDROMEDA: Yes. And when did you first see him?

HELOISE: I first saw him in the study at my uncle's house...and although we had never met before, he had seen me at the market and at church. He had been lecturing on the Holy Trinity when a reflection of light blinded his eyes. He turned and saw me. He said he had immediately fallen in love. I was beautiful then. I had long, dense hair–golden. The nuns made me shave it off when I joined the order. I used to wear jewels in my hair. That's what caught his eye, the jewels in my hair.

ANDROMEDA: And what—what happened?

(The light has now reached a blinding intensity.)

HELOISE: Abelard approached my uncle and offered his services to tutor me. He would teach the tenets of the Holy trinity while outlining the curve of my lips with his finger. I traced the outline of my breasts while reciting the Lords Prayer. We read the letters of Paul completely naked and quoted Revelations while fornicating. Soon, God and sex were combined in Abelard—and I could not pray without becoming wet. My uncle had never let me meet men before—so... Abelard was my savior.

ANDROMEDA: And then he took you away and you married—you eloped—you lied to your uncle and he was furious—and—and there was a *child*.

HELOISE: You didn't forget my story.

ANDROMEDA: It is beautiful. I could never forget it.

(The light slowly begins to diminish.)

HELOISE: My uncle said we were forgiven and could return, but then...the first moment Abelard was alone/

ANDROMEDA: /I don't like this part/

HELOISE: /My uncle got a group of men together and attacked Abelard in his sleep. The men restrained my love as my uncle tied a piece of twine around Abelard's parts and castrated him. *(A beat of disappointment.)* After that, Abelard didn't want to see me. He was ashamed. But I still loved him. I still wanted him.

ANDROMEDA: You still wanted him.

HELOISE: He left me and became a monk; told me to join the order. I became a nun...trapped with women...as I am now...because if I couldn't have Abelard, then I would remember him in prayer. I would pray and still become aroused. With every communion I would have a secret orgasm that was mine alone. I would feel him inside of me again. But I don't think he wanted me after that. No.

(Andromeda holds her.)

ANDROMEDA: He will come Heloise. He will. I believe that. Why else would we exist?

(The light has faded and is almost gone.)

HELOISE: I had beautiful hair. *(Beat)* Andromeda. *(She strokes Andromeda's cheek.)* I'm sorry I lied to you about the boat. There never was a light.

(The signal sounds for the third time, directly off stage. The other women of the island enter from all sides pointing with excitement and extreme agitation. Joan of Arc is brandishing a wicked sword. Cleopatra is bejeweled in red or purple, maintaining an eerie calm demeanor, slightly bemused by her situation and companions. Queen Victoria is an imposing figure of middle age, dressed in full mourning.)

VICTORIA: Where is it? Where is the boat?

HELOISE: There is no boat.

JOAN: But there is! God spoke to you and forewarned you correctly!

VICTORIA: Where's the light!

ANDROMEDA: There is no light!

CLEOPATRA *(calmly)*: The light's over there.

VICTORIA: Oh dear God!

ANDROMEDA: But we didn't see it! How—how—*how* could we not have seen it!

VICTORIA: It had to have passed right by you!

JOAN *(to the offstage boat)*: Here! I am here! I do not belong here!

HELOISE: We didn't see it.

ANDROMEDA: Oh Gods! Oh Gods, how could we not see?

21

CLEOPATRA: Nothing is going to bring that boat back.

ANDROMEDA: You can.

VICTORIA: If you really can do as you claim we wouldn't be waiting.

CLEOPATRA: No.

VICTORIA: You must.

CLEOPATRA: No.

VICTORIA: If you truly have the power, do it—do it now! The boat is leaving!

JOAN *(solemnly)*: I can do it. I can bring back the boat.

VICTORIA: Do it, Joan.

(Beat. We hear the call of the Hydra offstage. The women freeze.)

HELOISE: You're going to lose her forever if you send her into that water.

JOAN: As God is my witness, I shall.

HELOISE: If she goes in that water she really will die twice. She'll be fish food.

JOAN: The boat must take me where I belong.

(Joan marches into the water and swims offstage.)

ANDROMEDA: Heloise! Cleopatra! Don't you remember what happened to Sylvia?

CLEOPATRA: It was Joan who did that.

ANDROMEDA: I see a head!

CLEOPATRA: And there's another one.

ANDROMEDA: No!

HELOISE: Close your eyes.

CLEOPATRA: There's a tentacle.

VICTORIA: I command silence!

HELOISE: Oh! It's gonna come down on her.

ANDROMEDA: No!

(Joan's scream is heard off stage followed by the sound of something heavy hitting water.)

VICTORIA: Joan? Joan… The poor wretch is dead, God bless her soul.

ANDROMEDA: Look—

HELOISE: She's hanging off the Hydra's teeth!

CLEOPATRA: The sword of God may be dull but she's resilient.

ANDROMEDA: /Oh my gods, oh my gods, oh my gods!

HELOISE: /She's stabbing the Sea Monster with her sword!

CLEOPATRA: The boat is safe—look to the boat.

ANDROMEDA: Have you no feelings?

CLEOPATRA: Not for her.

HELOISE: There she is! She's nearing the boat!

CLEOPATRA: She's still alive—

VICTORIA: Joan! Joan! Turn back! You're leading the Hydra to the boat!

HELOISE and CLEOPATRA: Turn back! / Turn around! / No!

ANDROMEDA: She's at the boat!

HELOISE: Are you fucking kidding me?

ANDROMEDA: What? Ohhhhhh. Oh! Oh no!

(We hear the loud smack and the splintering of wood.)

HELOISE: Joan? Joan!

ANDROMEDA: Nothing. Just the shattered boat.

CLEOPATRA: The Hydra's…chewing…

ANDROMEDA: She can't die again.

CLEOPATRA: No, she'll just be trapped in the belly of the Hydra for the rest of eternity.

VICTORIA: There! Joan!

HELOISE: She's paddling towards us.

ANDROMEDA: She's pulling a bit of the wrecked boat!

HELOISE: There's someone on it! She saved someone!

VICTORIA: My Albert!

CLEOPATRA: It's not him.

VICTORIA: My Albert is coming for me.

CLEOPATRA: Unless Albert wears a dress it's not him on that raft.

ANDROMEDA: It's a woman. Just another woman.

(Heloise walks into the water and begins to wade off stage.)

VICTORIA: What are *you* doing?

HELOISE: Helping her.

(Cleopatra sits grandly, the entertainment over.)

ANDROMEDA: Oh. She's pretty. I thought you were so beautiful when you first came to this island.

CLEOPATRA: I still am beautiful.

(Heloise and Joan of Arc enter pulling a raft of splintered wood. Anaïs Nin sits atop a mountain of books. Her hair is dark and styled in a mid 1930's fashion. Joan leaves the raft and kneels before Victoria.)

JOAN: I fought the Hydra and brought back the passenger. God was not ready for me.

VICTORIA: Were there any others on the boat?

JOAN: The ferryman.

ANDROMEDA: The poor ferryman.

JOAN: I was filled by the power of God. He said, "Joan". He called my name. "Joan. This is God. I am going to enter you now". And so God entered me. And then God said, "Joan, you are going to fight the Sea Monster, but do not be afraid. For I shall be one with you." The sword in my hand was the sword of God and as I fought the Hydra I knew that God and I were fighting all of those who don't believe in him. I said, "God, I doubted you. You stranded me on this island and I doubted you. I expected to be in heaven with choirs of angels singing my rapturous praise instead of waiting for I know not what for. Alone with harlots, Jezebels, heretics, and British people." And then God said, "Joan, I forgive you, I love you. And as a reward, I shall tell you why you are here. Why you lived. Why you died." And then God released my mind and I heard him speak directly into my mind. I am the Chosen One! I am to know the secret of life! I am to know the ultimate answer! I am to know our purpose! And then He told me. God in his wisdom chose me to know, a peasant, a nothing I. And now I shall share his secret with all of you! God said, "Joan, you lived and died all because...I told you so." And now we know! Now you can believe! We suffered through life and the life after all because God said so! Isn't that beautiful?

(Anaïs reaches into her bag and pulls out a bottle of pills. She takes one out and pops it in Joan's mouth.)

ANAÏS: Swallow.

(Joan swallows.)

ANAÏS: Lithium…

VICTORIA: What year are you from?

ANAÏS: The late twentieth century—age of the post-modernists: people who sit around judging the choices of others without really doing anything themselves.

VICTORIA: Who are you?

ANAÏS: Anaïs Nin. Anna-is. It's *Anna* with an *ees*.

VICTORIA: I am Victoria, queen of England and this island of the dead.

ANDROMEDA: Andromeda, princess of Ethiopia and Greece.

HELOISE: Heloise.

CLEOPATRA: Cleopatra.

(Anaïs gasps, then runs to Cleopatra and lightly kisses her on the cheek.)

VOCTORIA: Yes… And you've met Joan.

(Joan sits and cleans her sword.)

ANAÏS: Are there only women on this island?

ANDROMEDA: Yes—I'm sorry—yes.

ANAÏS: Well that is a start! I asked to be taken as far away from men as possible.

VICTORIA: What impertinence. And they brought you here?

ANDROMEDA: No—It can't be—we are all waiting for our men.

CLEOPATRA: I wait for no man.

JOAN: I wait for God.

(Anaïs walks to the water and looks down at her reflection.)

HELOISE: How old were you when you died?

ANAÏS: Seventy-four. But I would say I look thirty-five now. It's lovely.

(She touches her face and then crosses to her pile of books—looking for one.)

CLEOPATRA: We think that you come back in the body you remember yourself most in.

ANAÏS: Yes.

HELOISE: What did you do in life, Anaïs?

ANAÏS: I was a writer.

HELOISE: Are these your books?

ANAÏS: These are my diaries.

ANDROMEDA: You lived all those books!

ANAÏS: Some is reality some is imagined—I could never tell the difference.

ANDROMEDA: Were you married?

ANAÏS: Twice.

JOAN: Whore.

VICTORIA: Why are you here?

ANAÏS: The little one swam out and dragged me here.

VICTORIA: You had two husbands—what was wrong with the first?

ANDROMEDA: Perhaps he died.

VICTORIA: Then she should have waited for him.

ANAÏS: My first husband didn't die. I was married to both at the same time—until I divorced one of them due to the complications bigamy inspires on one's taxes when two men try to claim you as a dependent.

VICTORIA: Get off this island.

ANAÏS: Is it yours?

HELOISE: You asked to be taken away from men. Why were you brought here?

CLEOPATRA: Did he intend for you to be here?

ANAÏS: Not at first…

ANDROMEDA: You mean there are other islands?

HELOISE: You know there are, like Karen's.

ANAÏS: Who?

VICTORIA: The Island of Karen Carpenter—just over there—we heard her singing/

CLEOPATRA: It felt like one sentenced to a thousand lashes—

ANDROMEDA: I love Karen Carpenter.

VICTORIA: We visited her. A lonely wretch.

HELOISE: She won't let you near her, just sits there gaunt and silent. She never speaks—

ANDROMEDA: She sings—I love her songs.

VICTORIA: I declared her mentally insane and we returned.

CLEOPATRA: But we have never seen or heard of other islands.

ANAÏS: There are several. None of them suited me.

ANDROMEDA: Were there only women on those islands as well?

ANAÏS: No. In fact one island only had one man.

VICTORIA: Who was he?

ANAÏS: Albert Camus. He lived after you.

ANDROMEDA: Tell us about him—I—I love stories.

ANAÏS: In the morning. I must sleep.

ANDROMEDA: You can sleep?

HELOISE: We have no morning. Only darkness.

JOAN: And we never sleep. We watch—we wait—we cannot sleep.

ANAÏS: It must be because we are closer.

JOAN: Closer to what?

ANAÏS: The mainland /

CLEOPATRA: Duat.

ANDROMEDA: Hades.

HELOISE: Hell.

JOAN: *Not Hell.*

HELOISE: We are. We are practically in Hell.

CLEOPATRA: Tell us about this Camus and his island. Is he dead? And there is still day?

ANAÏS: He is dead. And there is day. I was taken there—to his island—because I thought I wanted to be alone. Alone and away...alone. I assumed I would be taken to a deserted place but as we neared the island— a rock really, stretching miles into the sky— I met a tall, strikingly handsome man with hound dog eyes. I knew him immediately as Camus. He was brilliant and gorgeous—a man of legends and letters. I was ready to have him right there...but instead, he began to climb the cliff. I followed. Hours and hours of climbing and reaching and grasping—never getting closer—I could scream—I wanted him. Finally—we arrived at the top—his eyes were pleading. I was exhausted and my body was wet. I began to unbutton my dress. He maintained eye contact. He did not glance at my nipples. He did not blanch at the mound between my legs. He simply rushed at me...but before he reached me...he was finished... We dressed in silence. He started to cry. So I walked to the edge of the cliff and jumped. I hurled to the rocks and saw them race forward, knowing they would rip my body to pieces. And then, nothing. I had no thoughts. I disappeared. That is what I always assumed death would be. Darkness. You can imagine my disappointment when I awoke the next morning lying on that rock next to Camus. He asked if we could do it again. I was alone. The ferryman had done as I asked. Loneliness was just another man I could not lean on and I had to go on conquering myself alone. Eventually...I wondered if it was men. Maybe there is more to write about than this. In life I wrote this because no other woman had. But I don't like that language now. And I don't need it. *(She touches her diaries.)* These are not *me* anymore. I requested to be taken away from men entirely and forever.

(The women sit in silence and stare at Anaïs.)

VICTORIA: No one asks to be taken away from men.

ANDROMEDA: Is this what you wrote about?

ANAÏS: I wrote female erotica. I want to write new stories now.

ANDROMEDA: What is erotica?

ANAÏS: Sex.

ANDROMEDA: Sex?

(Victoria stiffens. Heloise grabs one of the books.)

ANAÏS: An old man paid me a dollar a page to write about sex. And I published it. I was the first woman.

HELOISE: Was it graphic—this sex—was it steamy?

(Joan sharpens her sword.)

ANAÏS: People thought of it as an insight to the mind through sex.

HELOISE: Were your books an insight to the mind?

ANAÏS *(wickedly)*: Who knows? I made a dollar a page. I had to prolong it. Start with a hair standing up. You feel it prickle in your womb germinating into a slow penetration with twists that make you gasp with pleasure. Sex can last for entire chapters.

HELOISE: If he has the equipment…

VICTORIA: Sister Heloise!

JOAN: A penis is just another sword men use to stab you with.

CLEOPATRA: For a man's pleasure, I would strip naked and rub oil all over my naked body.

HELOISE: That is *nice*.

CLEOPATRA: I shaved every inch of my-self...*naked*...after he saw that—a man didn't have to think any more. Sex is the lack of thought and the focus of action.

HELOISE: Fuck.

VICTORIA: Sister!

HELOISE: I used to masturbate with my rosary. I'd put it inside of me and pull it out—one—bead—at a—time—my lips would tense and—

ANDROMEDA: I have a confession to make—

HELOISE: I'm talking here!

JOAN: I have a sword! I have stabbed many men!

VICTORIA *(sternly)*: Joan—you're a girl.

JOAN *(defiantly)*: I am more of a man than most men.

ANDROMEDA: I'm a virgin! (*Beat*) I don't even know what sex is. Not really...

HELOISE: But you were married—

ANDROMEDA: I am unknown to man. I was engaged to my uncle—a nasty old man. On the day of our wedding, my mother made a vain comment about my beauty. She compared me to the gods—that's when it happened. An angry goddess came down and sentenced me to death—a virgin sacrifice fed to a ravenous Sea Monster and I hate Sea Monsters. But in a way I felt relieved. Instead of being fed to my lecherous uncle, I would be eaten alive by a giant reptile; it seemed like a fair trade. They stripped me of my clothes and tied me naked to a rock. (*She grabs onto two trees and writhes between them–reliving the event.*) The monster rose out of the blue gulf. A mix of saliva and surf covered me. Then—moments before the giant Sea Monster was to devour my virgin flesh—a man…a *man* flew through the air on a giant winged stallion to save me. My hero slaughtered the beast. He flew down on the ivory steed and said, "My name is Perseus and you will be my bride."

HELOISE: Then how can you be a virgin?

ANDROMEDA: I caught pneumonia from being strapped naked to a rock in the ocean. I died a week before my wedding–still a virgin. I am incomplete.

(Beat. Andromeda walks towards the water and wades in until she is waist deep. Heloise joins her and slowly holds her. A dim light shows Karen's island to the side. Karen timidly enters with a tambourine and begins the first beats of a song similar to "Superstar"—but changed. Some of this is sung and some may be spoken)

ANDROMEDA *(singing)*: Long ago, and oh so far away,
I fell in love with you when the Sea Monster died.
Your mandolin, it sounded so out of tune.
And then I died too soon. So, I attempt suicide.

HELOISE and ANDROMEDA: Don't you remember
you promised to love me baby?

KAREN: Ba ba ba ba ba ba ba ba

HELOISE and ANDROMEDA: When are you coming to
the Underworld baby?

KAREN: Ba ba ba ba ba ba ba ba

ANDROMEDA: Baby, Baby, Baby, Baby, Baby, Baby,
Baby, Baby, Baby, Baby, Baby/

(Heloise stops her.)

HELOISE: I love you. I really think I do.

(Victoria walks forward and joins them in the water.)

VICTORIA: Loneliness...is such a sad affair.
And I can hardly wait to rule over you again.
What to say to make you come again?
Be my subject again, and play your harpsichord.

VICTORIA and KAREN *(with tambourine)*: Don't
you—don't you--don't you--Don't you remember you
told me you loved me baby?
I'm ordering you to come back this way again baby?
Baby, Baby, Baby, Baby oh Baby, I love you. I really
do.

(Karen sits sadly and listens to Victoria—exiting after her speech.)

VICTORIA: We were not beautiful people. I am grateful for that blessing. We knew what it meant to love each other without question of it fading. I never wondered if he would tire of my face because there was nothing there of interest in the first place. He made me feel like a princess–and that's saying something considering I was already a queen. We were equals in intellect and wit, and...*family*. I remember every Christmas with the children. We both were so... He was greater to me than the empire. Albert, my Albert. And then he died. He left me to grow old alone. He missed seeing my wrinkles and my extra weight. I can hear the jokes he would have made about that. I suffered through the rest of my life without him and...he has to see what time did to me without him by my side. Albert my Albert. I cannot think of man without smelling his bad breath in the morning. I cannot use the word, "he". He. He. I cannot use that pronoun without it being about him in some way. And I have never said the word, "we", without fury after his death. We were happy. *(Beat. Then to Cleopatra.)* Tell me how you do it. Teach me.

CLEOPATRA: No.

JOAN: Sadness was supposed to lift with death. God always told me sadness was of the flesh. As I sat in the English prison waiting for the guards to take turns to try and rape me, He told me it would be better once I died.

(Anaïs feeds Joan another lithium pill.)

37

VICTORIA *(to Anaïs)*: If you wish to stay on this island there are certain rules. Without rules there would be no ruler and that is unacceptable to me—the Queen/

CLEOPATRA: *One* of the queens…

VICTORIA: The island is divided between Cleopatra, Queen of the polytheists, where she resides with Andromeda, and my side—Queen of the one true God, where everyone in structured attire lives. How many gods do you believe in? *(Beat. Anaïs has no appropriate answer.)* I understand it's confusing to modern women such as ourselves. As being part of my side of the island we have rules. First: Do not blaspheme.

CLEOPATRA: It upsets the Christians.

JOAN: I would gut you if she let me.

VICTORIA: The last woman who came here, Sylvia Plath, taught everyone wicked, modern words.

JOAN: Pussy, cock, cunt, clit.

VICTORIA: Second: no literature is allowed that has not passed the Censory Review Board.

ANAÏS: Who is the Censory Review Board?

VICTORIA: *I* am the Censory Review Board. Joan, confiscate her books. *(Joan goes to the raft and returns with the books.)* I have a library of selected and approved materials in my hut. It includes the Bible and the complete works of Jane Austin. The final and most important rule is this...do not ever turn away a man.

ANDROMEDA: It is the one rule that both sides share.

VICTORIA: Do you accept these terms?

ANAÏS: You have fed my ferryman to the Hydra and destroyed my boat.

VICTORIA: I'm so glad we understand each other. We alternate shifts here—one polytheist and one monotheist—to ensure fairness when a man does arrive. You shall team with Cleopatra. Farewell and good watching.

(Victoria and Joan exit with the books.)

ANDROMEDA: It's really not so bad. We all have the same purpose.

ANAÏS: What is that?

ANDROMEDA: To wait.

BLACKOUT

SCENE 2:

(Lights up as before, the scene is the same. Anaïs sits on the bank, staring out into the darkness. Cleopatra is lying on a large oriental rug with an array of cosmetics, mirrors, and fabrics surrounding her. She is painting her toenails with exacting precision.)

CLEOPATRA: Nefritiri preferred a ruby red. I lean more towards crimson. Your modern colors though are much less defined. Yet nuanced. This burgundy...are you a queen?

ANAÏS: No, of course not.

CLEOPATRA: Only queens were allowed to wear red in my court. You would be stripped.

ANAÏS: How tempting... In modern times, society serves each individual as his own king.

CLEOPATRA: How do you build a pyramid with a society of kings? No man would pull a brick. Have you seen anything? You're not going to. Nothing ever comes...

ANAÏS: Then, why do you? Why do you watch?

CLEOPATRA: It gives me time to do my nails. I stole this lip color from the island of Karen Carpenter. It's too pale. This mirror came with Heloise, but she didn't want it anymore. Sylvia Plath left behind this powder when she was fed to the Hydra.

ANAÏS: Why was she fed to the Hydra?

CLEOPATRA: She gave up. She wasn't waiting for anything. She was waiting for nothing—no she said she was waiting for "nothingness". Do you have anything to add to my collection?

ANAÏS: Do people always give you things?

CLEOPATRA: I am Isis in human form and one must pay tribute. (*Beat*) Is this where the ferryman intended you to be?

ANAÏS: Yes. Rid myself of men—now, I love men. I'm not a man-hater; I adore them. I just always wrote and thought about them. Do you think we could discover something new without them? That would be nice, yes? Get rid of the way they see us. Toss it out.

CLEOPATRA: You're like a child.

ANAÏS: Who are you waiting for?

CLEOPATRA: I'm not waiting for a *man*. If I wanted a man all I would have to do is walk up to that water, touch my toe to the surface, call out—and he would swim to me.

ANAÏS (*innocently seductive*): So you are waiting for a woman?

CLEOPATRA: I'm waiting for a child.

ANAÏS: A child…

CLEOPATRA: My son. They were going to kill him in front of me. I died to save him.

ANAÏS: They did kill him. He died alone.

CLEOPATRA: That is why I wait for him. In life I wanted a son so that I could raise him to rule a man's world
as a man. I chose his father for the *man* that he was.
And we had a son. Both of us—Dictator and Goddess
shared something human and created a child. We
could never be together—but our son… I was even
pregnant with a second when he died. The moment I
was told—your Caesar is dead, his child died in my
womb… But that would not stop me. No, I created a
God in my living son. And he would be a great man;
everything his parents could never be. But now. I
wish I had him, just to see him laugh, hear his voice,
touch his hair—to be mother and son again.

ANAÏS: You remind me of someone I knew in life.

CLEOPATRA: She must have been beautiful. Everyone
says I remind them of someone and she is always
beautiful—but was she wise?

ANAÏS: She was strong. She was the wife of one of my
lovers. My most dangerous lover.

CLEOPATRA: She must have hated you.

ANAÏS: No.

CLEOPATRA: I should learn your magic.

ANAÏS: She was also my lover.

CLEOPATRA: Ah…

ANAÏS: Here.

(Anaïs rubs lotion on her feet.)

CLEOPATRA: Yes.

ANAÏS: But I couldn't commit to it.

CLEOPATRA: No?

ANAÏS: I thought that if I did—I would become like a man and dominate her as a man to a woman. I would lose my softness. Also I had no penis.

CLEOPATRA: No.

ANAÏS: I think now…I would simply kiss her from love. I would attempt a more subtle penetration with the eyes, hands and senses that only a woman has. Have you ever been intimate with a woman? *(Beat. Cleopatra is still. Tension. Anaïs sees a discarded hourglass. She picks it up playfully.)* Play a game with me! Here! As long as the sand is running, we are not to mention a man by name, pronoun, or reference of any kind!

CLEOPATRA: Why?

ANAÏS: An experiment.

CLEOPATRA: It won't be difficult.

ANAÏS: I agree!

(She turns the clock over and the sand begins to run.)

CLEOPATRA: A like mind is what *I* miss most. Some-one who thinks as I do. All of us from different times—none of us will ever look at the trees and see the same picture—or read a word and have in it the same meaning. That is what *queens* are for: an image for each person to look at and say—that is me—I think as *her* and feel as *her*. I do not care for individuals—I care for culture. As symbolized by a queen.

ANAÏS: Yes.

CLEOPATRA: I would like to read your books. I had a library once, destroyed by the wars. In it were the most remarkable plays—sciences too—books on as-tronomy and—yes, my people even knew the world was round centuries before the Western World and Monotheists caught up. The people of the goddess Isis knew. But it was all lost. *(She studies her.)* I wonder at one who thought to write about herself and not the world around her.

ANAÏS: I write to taste life twice. *(Anaïs hands her a book.)* It is a very intimate act: to ask to read my thoughts.

CLEOPATRA: They are all you brought with you so they must be a symbol—a talisman of who you are.

ANAÏS: What did you bring?

CLEOPATRA: This rug. This old thing that has been with me since I was seventeen.

ANAÏS: Really?

CLEOPATRA: I remember dying. I remember that. And then the next thing I know...I'm on a dock being guided onto a boat. I step in and sit on this. Old rug. This is the rug that saved my life—

ANAÏS: Yes?

CLEOPATRA: Do you always do that?

ANAÏS: What?

CLEOPATRA: Speak one word at a time? Do you ever use a complete sentence?

ANAÏS: Sometimes... *(She opens her purse and pulls out a lipstick)* You can have this color red if you let me put it on you.

CLEOPATRA: Good. I have been waiting for an attendant.

ANAÏS: I have to wipe this off before I can put on the new color. *(Anaïs gently begins to wipe off Cleopatra's lipstick.)*

CLEOPATRA: Who are you waiting for?

ANAÏS *(playfully proud)*: I don't need anyone. I am a migratory bird. It's true! That's why I keep going island to island to island.

CLEOPATRA: I'm searching for the perfect shade of red.

ANAÏS: When I was sixteen, I quit school to begin modeling. My first job was to pose for a portrait of you.

CLEOPATRA: You look nothing like me.

ANAÏS: People think you're white.

CLEOPATRA: What!

ANAÏS: Everyone. Pucker your lips. They even made a movie—a moving picture—with a white woman. A lot of make-up though.

CLEOPATRA: Well the make-up…

ANAÏS: All images of the actual you have been destroyed. So they had to invent one. You died a mother to be painted by time as a whore. The world doesn't live with your true image—as you have—as you've never changed. I think this red will suit you.

(Anaïs finishes with the lipstick. The sands of time have run out.)

ANAÏS: Our time is finished! That wasn't long at all.

(Cleopatra turns it over again.)

CLEOPATRA: I think we can do better.

(Anaïs joyfully claps her hands.)

ANAÏS: Yes! If this is hell, hell is heaven!

CLEOPATRA: You really get excited about yourself, don't you?

ANAÏS: Reality never impressed me. I only believe in intoxication, in ecstasy!

CLEOPATRA: You never had children.

ANAÏS *(happily)*: Only abortions and books.

CLEOPATRA: Having a child is a completely different kind of love.

ANAÏS: All love is incest. We only love in others what we love about ourselves.

CLEOPATRA: Death has been more real to me than life ever was.

ANAÏS: Yes! There are no rules—no systems—no countries with lines and everyone trying to conquer and conquer and conquer! We are all just…melting clocks waiting to be ourselves and not be mounted on a wall!

CLEOPATRA: We don't have to fight to be who we are! I wait for my son—

ANAÏS: No. *(Beat)* No! You blew it! No!

(Anaïs knocks over the hourglass.)

CLEOPATRA: I did not mention a man—

ANAÏS: Your *son*—

CLEOPATRA: A child is not a man.

ANAÏS: But it still reduces who you are. The love between women is a refuge and an escape into harmony. You are a "lover" or a "mother" whenever a man is brought into the conversation. Let's edit them out for a while and let them back in later if they behave.

CLEOPATRA: Don't paint your own demons in my face. I know who I am.

ANAÏS: Look at you disagreeing with me.

CLEOPATRA: No one dictates to a queen.

ANAÏS: I find your stubbornness very appealing.

(Anaïs leans in to kiss Cleopatra, but is stopped when a loud noise is heard off stage. It begins as a battle cry.)

CLEOPATRA: Not again!

ANAÏS: Do you see a boat?

CLEOPATRA: The last time they sounded the drums they got rid of Sylvia. We have to hide you.

ANAÏS: Me?

CLEOPATRA: All I have to do is whisper and a man would swim here.

ANAÏS: Really?

CLEOPATRA: If I wanted to, I could call their men to them in a moment.

ANAÏS: So it is me…

CLEOPATRA: Quick! Look for a place to hide.

ANAÏS: No. This should be fun.

(Cleopatra grabs the Oriental rug and lifts it in the air.)

CLEOPATRA: When my brother was trying to assassinate me, I twisted myself up in this rug and had it delivered as a gift to Caesar. He uncoiled it to find a girl: cornered, sweating, and half naked–but unafraid. We were lovers that night.

ANAÏS: I'm not frightened of them—

CLEOPATRA: If I have to spend an eternity trapped with any person; it should be you.

ANAÏS: Yes!

CLEOPATRA: Get in the rug.

(Anaïs lies in the rug. Cleopatra rolls her up so it lands down stage. She sits on the rug just as Heloise and Andromeda enter.)

ANDROMEDA: What's happening? Did you tell her to go? She—she has to leave!

CLEOPATRA: She's swimming away right now.

ANDROMEDA: What has Anaïs done?

HELOISE: Victoria probably got half way through one of Anaïs' books. You remember what happened to Silvia? All cut up into little pieces...each alive and conscience...fed one by one to the Hydra. Her last words were: "At last...the bell jar!"

(Joan enters swinging a battle-axe. Victoria follows her with a book.)

VICTORIA: Filth! Gross Indecency! This is dreadful!

JOAN: She has ruined me!

HELOISE: What has she written that's so terrible?

VICTORIA: Here! In this book! "The Delta of Venus"

ANDROMEDA: Is that a river?

HELOISE: It sounds more like a metaphor.

JOAN: Ruined me!

VICTORIA: It is filth! Listen! "She closed her eyes and thought: Now he is lifting my dress slowly, very slow-ly. He is looking at me first. One hand slides over my buttocks, and the other begins exploring, sliding, cir-cling. Now he dips his finger in there, where it is moist." I can read no further. I dare not.

HELOISE: No-no–read some more.

VICTORIA: "The presence of his hand aroused her more than ever. Then she would close her eyes again and try to imagine his hand was moving. To create a suffi-ciently vivid image for herself, she would begin to contract and open her vagina, rhythmically, until she felt the orgasm."

ANDROMEDA: How do you open your vagina without touching it?

VICTORIA: No woman should ever be forced to read this.

HELOISE: I'm a nun used to making sacrifices. Allow me to finish reading it for you.

JOAN: Where is she! Where did she go!

VICTORIA: The wretch must be punished.

CLEOPATRA: She swam away.

JOAN: No! No—no—no—she couldn't have got away. She couldn't. I must have vengeance.

CLEOPATRA: I heard the signal, told her what happened to Sylvia and she fled.

JOAN: No!

VICTORIA: It doesn't matter now.

JOAN: No! No! (*Joan drops to the ground in severe distress.*) He's gone! He's gone forever!

ANDROMEDA: Joan?

HELOISE: Stay back.

VICTORIA: Joan. Get up this instant.

JOAN: Speak to me! Tell me what to do! I don't know what to do!

VICTORIA: I am telling you what to do. Get up.

JOAN: Please. Please.

(*Andromeda runs to Joan.*)

JOAN: Keep away from me.

(Andromeda kneels down and cradles Joan.)

ANDROMEDA: What's wrong, Joan?

JOAN: It's gone forever.

ANDROMEDA: What's gone Joan?

JOAN: The voice of God is gone. It's disappeared. He's left me. God has left me. I must have failed him. It started after she gave me that thing.

VICTORIA: That pill.

JOAN: Yes. And after that, He left me. I first heard Him when I was a little girl. But I knew in my soul…I knew I wasn't a girl. I wasn't the sex they told me I had to be. I was stronger than they ever knew. I was not what they called me. But God, He always told me what I was, what to do. When he told me I was a man; I was a man, if he said kill; I'd kill. When he told me to fight, I would fight. Life was simple. I would do what I was told. But now…I don't know what to do. Where is He? I am alone. I am alone.

VICTORIA: Joan.

JOAN: What did I do? He left me. He left me. What did I do wrong? Without His voices, I am not special. Who am I if I am not chosen? I thought I was special. Alone. Alone. Alone.

(Joan cries her self to sleep. The women watch in horror.)

ANDROMEDA: Joan. Joan? Heloise! Something has happened to Joan.

HELOISE: She is asleep. Let her sleep.

ANDROMEDA: We can't sleep.

HELOISE: She's asleep, Andromeda.

ANDROMEDA: We aren't allowed to sleep.

HELOISE: We are put on this island to wait. Her hope is gone.

(Victoria kneels down beside Joan.)

CLEOPATRA *(to Victoria)*: You've lost your soldier.

ANDROMEDA: Leave her alone.

CLEOPATRA: Anaïs deserves a medal.

ANDROMEDA: She took away Joan's God—Joan's hope!

HELOISE: It was false.

ANDROMEDA: Who are you to judge another person's God or its validity?

CLEOPATRA: Of everything in your histories I have seen—the Christian God is the most destructive— devoid of anything human—a religion of chains and not a celebration of life.

ANDROMEDA: No one deserves to have their spirit taken away.

CLEOPATRA: She did.

ANDROMEDA: No one can judge another person's beliefs.

CLEOPATRA: I can, because I know that I am right.

(Victoria picks up Joan's axe.)

VICTORIA: Where is she?

CLEOPATRA: …

VICTORIA: I've spent over a century with you. An eternity of having to listen how you slept with your servants, how you had sex with kings, how you slept with your brother. *(Anaïs gasps from inside the rug.)* I also remember how you escaped to those kings.

(Victoria kicks the rug. It unrolls and reveals Anaïs.)

ANAÏS: You really slept with your brother? I slept with my father—so much to discuss!

VICTORIA: An end to this!

ANAÏS: Victoria, if I could I would run my tiny hands inside you—coiling upwards and finally cracking your skull to massage your mind until it opened and accepted the possibility of life with magic.

(Victoria raises the axe.)

CLEOPATRA: Stop! *(Beat)* I'll do as you wish. *(Beat)* I'll call a man to this island.

ANDROMEDA: Heloise, she said a *man*–

VICTORIA: What?

HELOISE: Can you really call a man?

(Victoria lowers the axe.)

ANAÏS: Don't do this for me. Don't do this to us.

(Cleopatra walks downstage, towards the water.)

ANDROMEDA: Who will you call for?

VICTORIA: She will call for my Albert.

HELOISE: Why not my Abelard? Or Andromeda's? She's been here the longest.

ANDROMEDA: Why not her own?

CLEOPATRA: I will call for any man. Whoever is willing to come, will come.

(Cleopatra turns to the water. She walks until she is waist deep. Through this, Karen Carpenter slowly creeps onstage to witness the events. Cleopatra spreads her hands over the surface and closes her eyes. She lifts her head to the sky and opens her mouth. Suddenly, she falls underwater and is completely submerged. The women gasp and move to the edge. Anaïs stays on the rug, watching. After a moment, Cleopatra rises. She flings her dark hair back. She returns to the shore and lies next to Anaïs.)

HELOISE: Did anyone hear you?

VICTORIA: No one's coming.

ANDROMEDA: But he must! He must come.

HELOISE: Perhaps it wouldn't be so bad, Andromeda–if they never came.

VICTORIA: She's been lying to us forever—

HELOISE: There!

VICTORIA: What?

HELOISE: There is something in the water!

ANDROMEDA: Not again, Heloise.

HELOISE: Look! Can't you see it? There is someone in the water.

ANDROMEDA: There is! There is someone swimming!

VICTORIA: Nonsense.

HELOISE: Oh my God!

VICTORIA: There's nothing out there.

HELOISE: There is! There. Can't you see?

ANDROMEDA: I do! I see!

HELOISE: I see it!

ANDROMEDA: I see it!

VICTORIA: I see something. I see it!

(Cleopatra stands and looks off shore.)

ANDROMEDA: Is it a man or a woman?

HELOISE: I can't tell.

ANDROMEDA: Please, please.

HELOISE: It's a man.

ANDROMEDA: It is.

VICTORIA: As Queen of England and therefore this island, I declare that there is a man off shore!

ANDROMEDA: He's swimming right towards us!

VICTORIA: As Queen of England and therefore this island, I declare I shall be the first to greet him!

(Victoria hikes up her gown and runs into the water and off stage.)

ANDROMEDA: No! No! I should be first!

(Andromeda grabs Heloise by the arm and they run into the water.)

ANAÏS: Don't you see that this is a paradise? A wonder-
ful experiment—a group of women without the voice
of man.

CLEOPATRA: Did you know that would happen to
Joan? That she would fall asleep. That you would
destroy her?

ANAÏS: I wanted her to see as we see. I am not evil.

CLEOPATRA: There's a man off that shore. And he could lead me to my child.

ANAÏS: But that isn't what you need. I know what you need.

(Cleopatra exits. Anaïs sees Karen.)

KAREN: If it's my husband I'll never sing again.

(She hurries back to her island.)

ANDROMEDA: Anaïs! Look! We found a man.

BLACKOUT

ACT TWO: *THE MEN ARRIVE*

SCENE 1:

(Same as end of Act One. Victoria, Cleopatra, Heloise, and Andromeda enter carrying Lord Alfred "Bosie" Douglas. He is a young man in his early twenties with blonde hair and fair skin. He is drenched and unconscious.)

ANDROMEDA: Anaïs! Look! We found a man.

(They lay Bosie on the ground. Heloise straddles his body. She puts her fists together and pounds on his chest.)

VICTORIA: Give him room! Spread out!

(Heloise continues to pound on Bosie's chest.)

ANDROMEDA: Isn't he handsome? He has nice eyes– light. I saw them before he fainted. You know, I think he was frightened of us. He was swimming to- wards the island, lifted his head, opened his eyes and saw us approaching—four women, wet and succulent. And he screamed. He let out this high-pitched squeal and turned around. He started swimming in the other direction. That's when Victoria picked up a rock and smashed it in his head.

(Cleopatra indicates it is her turn. Heloise moves back and Cleopatra straddles Bosie. She leans down and gen- tly kisses Bosie on the lips, deeply.)

VICTORIA: Christ have mercy.

ANDROMEDA: She has an advantage.

CLEOPATRA: Nothing. He's not responding.

HELOISE: Are we sure it's a man?

ANDROMEDA: Of course it is.

CLEOPATRA: Maybe he's a eunuch.

VICTORIA: I'll be the judge of this.

(Victoria gets down and grabs Bosie's crotch. He screams.)

VICTORIA: Everything is there!

BOSIE: That bitch just grabbed my balls!

ANDROMEDA: She was making sure that all was as it should be.

BOSIE: That was highly inappropriate.

HELOISE: Can I get you anything?

ANDROMEDA: I want to get him something!

BOSIE: A nice glass of wine would be fabulous.

HELOISE: We don't have any wine.

BOSIE: Then why did you ask?

CLEOPATRA: Throw him back.

BOSIE: Where is he? Is he here?

ANDROMEDA: Are you looking for someone?

VICTORIA: I thought you were going to call a man?

CLEOPATRA: I did call a man.

VICTORIA: Next time be more specific.

BOSIE: Oscar! Oscar! Are you here!

ANDROMEDA: Who is Oscar?

BOSIE: My special friend.

ANDROMEDA: There are no men here.

BOSIE: No men!?!

ANDROMEDA: Except for you, maybe.

VICTORIA: Allow me to introduce myself–

BOSIE: Oh, I know who you are, Vicki.

VICTORIA: I am sure you are honored to meet me.

BOSIE: Oh poor big old Vicki's
    Parts never get sticky.
    'Tis rumored her clitoris is fried.
    Her husband is dead
    From boredom 'tis said
    And God knows that he's never lied.
    ... I'm a poet.

VICTORIA: What is this?

BOSIE: I know you, Vicki. And you know me.

VICTORIA: Who are you?

BOSIE: I am Lord Alfred Douglas.

ANDROMEDA: Charming.

BOSIE: My friends call me Bosie.

VICTORIA: Off! Throw him off! Get this disgrace out of here!

BOSIE: I will not allow you to judge me twice. You judged me in life, bitch, but not in death.

HELOISE: What was your crime?

BOSIE: I partake of the love that dare not speak its name.

HELOISE: Oh.

ANDROMEDA: What?

ANAÏS: He sleeps with men.

VICTORIA: Gross Indecency.

CLEOPATRA: Some people like to sleep with men…

VICTORIA: Alright! That's it! The lovemaking in my life was more than adequate. My Albert was a lover of immense proportions and he pleasured me deeply. I have stifled that fact for centuries as I am not a boastful woman and you are all filthy minded, but he knew what he was doing—*down there...* I had *nine* children and not because I like children.

CLEOPATRA: Well...he feels the same way.

ANDROMEDA: Back home, the men were married to women, but their lovers were all men.

BOSIE: Where are *you* from?

ANDROMEDA: Greece.

BOSIE: The Greeks really knew what was going on. Men are superior to women. Therefore, the most appropriate lover for a man is another man.

ANAÏS: Is this what you wanted?

BOSIE: Homosexual men are a superior breed to heterosexual men. We have evolved.

ANAÏS: You're still aggressive. You have no idea what it's like to be feminine.

BOSIE: Yes I do and anyone who says it doesn't hurt is lying. Can someone give me a massage? I have been swimming for a very long time.

VICTORIA: None of us are servants here. We are fine bred or wealthy; some of us are even queens.

BOSIE: Are you insinuating that I am a queen?

VICTORIA: I most certainly am not.

BOSIE: A little effeminate perhaps, but definitely not a queen. I object.

VICTORIA: Just sit down for a moment until we decide what to do with you.

BOSIE: You say there are no other men on this island?

ANDROMEDA: You are the only man.

BOSIE: Then it's clear my Oscar is not here. I'm not staying.

ANDROMEDA: You're not staying?

BOSIE: Of course not. This is not what I want.

HELOISE: But this is what you have.

BOSIE: So what...you sit around and wait for something else?

ANDROMEDA: We wait for our lives to return to us.

BOSIE: You wait for your Albert, I suppose.

VICTORIA: ...

BOSIE: What is the sense in living if you aren't fighting for something—getting what you want?

ANAÏS: You'll never find your answer in someone else.

BOSIE: My answer is someone else. Do you know what it's like–to disappear...no–not disappear–to join as one individual with another individual and create something else...another person?

VICTORIA: To become a "we".

BOSIE: Yes. We became a "we". It was just for a moment. For a split-second—I would die for Oscar Wilde. He was being taken to prison. He was moments away from being arrested for sodomy—for loving me. For fighting. And he chose to fight for me rather than run away. We were in his hotel room. He could easily have fled, but he chose to fight *society's* gross indecency. He chose to fight for me. And I kissed him. I kissed him deeply and blended into him. In that moment I knew I could never leave him. I would never abandon him. We were together for eternity. And then...in the next moment...the next moment I left... I left. The moment was over and I did abandon him.

ANAÏS: We're never truly the same person from one moment to the next.

BOSIE: Which is horse-shit. Oscar was the same way—always mewling about and never acting. Always thinking about other worlds. Well this is now. I am now! And I am going to swim to every island in hell if I have to so that I can find him.

HELOISE: So you're just jumping back in now? Swimming away?

BOSIE: Yes.

ANDROMEDA: You can't!

BOSIE: This time I am going to prove to Oscar that I am willing to fight for him also.

VICTORIA: What if we want to go with you? Theoreti-
cally, you disgust me. Homosexuals disgrace the
name of marriage, women, and family. But personal-
ly, I like your style. I am exceptionally fair; even if I
don't respect you—I still like you.

BOSIE: I respect that.

VICTORIA: I am sick of waiting! Do you think I waited
for Albert to propose?

ALL: No.

VICTORIA: No! Of course not! I *told* him! I can't believe I have waited around this long.

ANDROMEDA: Are we Heloise? Are we really going to
find them?

BOSIE: It always takes a man to motivate action.

CLEOPATRA: Usually without thinking first. But yes.
I'm going.

VICTORIA: We are all going.

ANAÏS: No.

VICTORIA: Good, I hate writers. They always think
they know the ending.

ANAÏS: There is no end.

VICTORIA: There is always an end—and yours will be
spent alone.

BOSIE: So are we on? Are we going now?

ANDROMEDA: You expect me to swim in that water?

VICTORIA: Anaïs' boat! We have a boat! We'll repair it. Cut down some trees…yes!

ANDROMEDA: Yes! Yes!

(Anaïs begins to exit through the trees.)

VICTORIA: Where are you going?

ANAÏS: To find my journals.

(Anaïs exits.)

ANDROMEDA: No. Someone needs to wait here. We can't all leave the post.

VICTORIA: Anaïs told the ferryman to bring her to an island where no man would follow–no offence to Lord Douglas–

BOSIE: Thank you.

VICTORIA: Well she can have it, but we will not settle for that fate. We will not be alone.

BLACKOUT

SCENE 2:

(Same as before. Only now, a bundle of Birch tree trunks lie center stage. The set is clear except for Joan of Arc, asleep near the upstage trees. Heloise is alone in a corner of the stage reading Delta of Venus. Karen is on her island, nervously studying the shore. Anaïs enters with her pile of books and dumps them center stage. Karen begins to leave.)

ANAÏS: You can come out now. It's safe. It wasn't him. *(Karen stops. Anaïs picks up a book.)* Want a read? *(Karen shakes her head.)* Me either. *(Anaïs tosses the book in the water.)* He hit you? *(Karen nods.)* I hate men who are afraid of women's strength. *(Beat)* Will you sing for me? *(Karen shrugs. Shakes her head.)* Please.

(Karen struggles with what to sing. She slowly plays the melody to what should be a happy song. She stops. Then without music, sings.)

KAREN *(sung)*: He won't let me smile without him.
　　He won't let me smile without him.
　　Won't let me laugh,
　　Won't let me sleep,
　　I can't even talk to people I meet.

　　I should feel sad if he's sad.
　　And feel glad if he's glad.
　　You must know what I'm goin' though.
　　I just can't smile without him.

　　(Spoken) I knew him for four months. I thought I had finally broken through—life—that it made sense. I struggled my entire life. To relax—trust—live—to

68

eat. It wasn't new. But I could control it. Then... You feel as if your life is nothing but highs and lows based on him. You study him, get to know what every twitch and silence might mean. My emotions became his property. My voice—his as well. There were times I couldn't sing. They are the moments before he hits you that are the most terrifying. When it's happening, it's just happening. So I stopped singing. And I stopped eating. And I stopped breathing. In life I sang words other people wrote for me. Now I'm changing them.

ANAÏS: Yes?

KAREN *(sung)*: I feel sad if I'm sad.
    I feel glad if I'm glad.
    And you must know what I'm goin' through.
    I can smile with out him.

(Karen smiles and exits. Heloise has stood and joined and holds her hand. Beat.)

ANAÏS: Finished with the raft?

HELOISE *(hiding the book)*: It won't take much longer.

ANAÏS: You must be happy to leave...

HELOISE: Yes.

ANAÏS: I'm happy for you.

HELOISE: Add it do the pile... *(She pulls out the book.)* It's one of yours.

ANAÏS: Did you like it?

HELOISE: Dirty girl… *(She grins.)* Your women will do anything.

ANAÏS: As long as it is their choice.

(Heloise hands her the book.)

ANAÏS: You keep it.

HELOISE: It's your life's work.

ANAÏS: If there is a hell, it is being reminded of who you've been in the past. It is your past. You are past. I am sick of being defined by who I was.

HELOISE: Aren't you proud of who you were?

ANAÏS: I thought that owning sex—liking sex would free me. But I was still tied to a man—in every moment! Everything I believed in was false. Do you know what that's like?

HELOISE: Look at me. *(Beat.)* Anaïs, I've been waiting for a man who didn't love me. In life he never came for me. Why would he now? You know, I enjoyed thinking about him more that I did our actual time together? I loved to imagine him coming for me. Secretly it was him I prayed to.

ANAÏS: I've done that.

HELOISE: No, you haven't. He never loved me. Not as I did. He never fucking loved me.

ANAÏS: You aren't leaving. At least I hope not. Stay. *(Beat)* You want to ask him why he never came? What does it matter?

HELOISE: Ah fuck it.

ANAÏS: Yes!

HELOISE: Fine. Fuck it! Fuck *him*!

ANAÏS: Yes! Fuck him!

HELOISE: He never had any balls. I mean, Anaïs, he had no balls! *(They laugh wickedly.)* Fuck all of it!

(Anaïs pulls off Heloise's wimple that has been tightly fastened about her head and a beautiful abundance of yellow hair drapes down around her face. She gasps and throws her body back onto the sand. She touches her hair with both hands and combs through it with her fingers. She crawls back to the water and looks at her reflection. She ceremoniously takes off her rosary from around her neck and places it in the sand beside her. She then unbuttons her top and pulls down her black dress so that her shoulders are bare. She looks in the water. She is beautiful. Heloise begins to laugh.)

ANAÏS: Look. Look.

HELOISE *(laughing hysterically)*: I don't know why it is so funny… but it is... I am beautiful… just like in the stories I tell Andromeda.

ANAÏS: You are so beautiful.

HELOISE: I don't *need* him now.

ANAÏS: People see it as a weakness…the depth a woman can feel. I see it as strength.

HELOISE: Andromeda always said I was beautiful. Andromeda... Andromeda will never stay.

ANAÏS: She might if you ask her.

HELOISE: Why would she stay for me?

ANAÏS: She loves you.

HELOISE: ...

ANAÏS: I have had many lovers—I've never had a friend...and I know the way a woman touches her lover. Speaks of her lover.

HELOISE: Oh.

ANAÏS: You love her.

HELOISE: ...

ANAÏS: From the boat, I saw two women on shore. One was holding the other in her lap. I knew they were lovers. And when I met them...I saw they did not know it yet.

HELOISE: Oh.

ANAÏS: Yes.

HELOISE: Yes... Yes... Yes...

ANAÏS: But you cannot search for answers in her.

HELOSIE: I am not searching for something in her. I think I found it in her. I love her! I love *her*.

ANAÏS: You always have.

HELOISE: Yes. Thank you. Yes.

ANAÏS: Make her stay with us.

HELOISE: How?

ANAÏS: We create our moments.

(Beat. Anaïs squeezes her hand and exits. Heloise stares at her reflection, laughing wildly and crying. Andromeda enters through the trees with difficulty. She is pulling a large birch tree. She waddles backwards and trips onto the sand. This makes Heloise laugh harder. Andromeda turns and sees her.)

ANDROMEDA: Heloise!

HELOISE: Don't come any closer!

(Heloise begins to button her blouse and put her wimple over her head. Andromeda runs to her and stops her.)

HELOISE: Let me put it back on.

ANDROMEDA: You always said they made you shave your head.

HELOISE: I did. They did shave it.

ANDROMEDA: When you were on the boat, didn't you check to see if it was back?

HELOISE: I came back dressed as a nun…

ANDROMEDA: It's beautiful.

HELOISE: I was so fixed in the memory that I continued to live in it.

ANDROMEDA: Just how I imagined it. Every time you told the story—my bedtime story. I can really see you now–as he saw you. I can see you truly, as he did. Walking from your church. He saw you in the sunlight that day—but the moonlight is just as beautiful.

HELOISE: Now can you see why he loved me?

ANDROMEDA: I always understood. You are *Heloise*.

HELOISE: He fell in love with my beauty.

ANDROMEDA: Then he never truly loved you.

HELOISE: No!

ANDROMEDA: Well, maybe he did.

HELOISE: No.

ANDROMEDA: Not as I do.

(Andromeda runs her fingers through Heloise's hair and kisses her gently.)

HELOISE: Yes.

ANDROMEDA: You are my Heloise, my protector. You take care of me.

HELOISE: I also make fun of you.

ANDROMEDA: Yes.

HELOISE: Do you think that it's true? What Anaïs says? That we are never the same person from one moment to the next.

ANDROMEDA: I don't know what that means. I've never been anyone but myself. I love you.

(Andromeda kisses Heloise.)

HELOISE: That's nice.

ANDROMEDA: Women are soft. Men are always rough to touch. Rough to kiss. They bite.

HELOISE: I can bite.

ANDROMEDA: That's not what I meant.

HELOISE *(whispering)*: I have one of Anaïs' books…

ANDROMEDA: Read to me!

HELOISE: You can read it yourself when I'm done.

ANDROMEDA: No. Read to me. Read me please. When you speak, I see things more clearly. When you say words—I listen.

HELOISE: All right. Are you sure you can take it? Yes. "How the honey flowed from her. He dipped his fingers in it lingeringly, then his sex, then he moved her so that she lay on him/"

ANDROMEDA: Oh.

HELOISE: "Her legs thrown over his legs"

ANDROMEDA: I never thought of that.

HELOISE: "And as he took her, he could see himself entering into her, and she could see him too. They saw their bodies undulate together –"

ANDROMEDA: Shit. *(She gasps.)*

HELOISE: "Seeking their climax. He was waiting for her, watching her movements. Because she did not quicken her movements, he changed her position, making her lie back."

ANDROMEDA: How would you do that?

HELOISE: Here, I'll show you. *(She demonstrates on top of Andromeda)* "He crouched over so that he could take her with more force, touching the very bottom of her womb, touching the very flesh walls again and again, and then she experienced the sensation that within her womb some new cells awakened/"

ANDROMEDA: What would awaken!?!

HELOISE: "New fingers. New mouths, that they responded to his entrance and joined in their rhythmic motion, that this suction would become gradually more and more pleasurable—"

ANDROMEDA: Wait...I can't!

HELOISE: What?

ANDROMEDA: Will we still be friends?

HELOISE: What do you mean?

ANDROMEDA: Whenever friends make love, they say the friendship dies.

HELOISE: We haven't made love.

ANDROMEDA: Isn't that what we are doing?

HELOISE: No.

ANDROMEDA: I thought it was.

HELOISE: We haven't made love, yet.

ANDROMEDA: Oh.

HELOISE: And when we do...you will know me. Not in the way men know me. Because you already know who Heloise is—Who I am—most do not wait to know–they escape in the body. I release you into the body.

ANDROMEDA: That sounds nice.

HELOISE: Yes.

(They kiss deeply.)

ANDROMEDA: We will still be friends? When I have found Perseus and you have found Abelard?

HELOISE: Oh.

ANDROMEDA: They say people disappear into another person when they become a couple. I don't want to lose you. Just because I find my man doesn't mean I still can't have you. My man is what I expected. You are the unexpected prize to go with it.

HELOISE: I always am an idea to my lover. Never myself.

ANDROMEDA: I like to hear you speak—even when I don't understand what you're saying. It's like a lullaby.

(Andromeda kisses Heloise.)

HELOISE: Andromeda, we could stay.

ANDROMEDA: There are no rules. You are dead. Are you in heaven? Do you see what was taught in your religion? Is this their afterlife? Is there a God, or angels, or Saint Piper?

HELOISE: Peter.

ANDROMEDA: Peter.

HELOISE: I gave up on religion centuries ago.

ANDROMEDA: Oh no religion is real, yours is just wrong. Look around… I was taught to believe in Hydras, and the River Styx, and eternal existence under the world. It seems like I had it right all along.

(Heloise kisses Andromeda. She tosses her rosary into the sea.)

HELOISE: Will you protect me too? Please.

ANDROMEDA: I think you should leave your hair down.

HELOISE: So do I.

(They kiss.)

ANDROMEDA: We should go and bring more trees.

HELOISE: No. Let's stay here. I'll read you some more.

ANDROMEDA: Come with me…

(They exit. After a beat, Anaïs enters with more books and drops them on her pile. She begins to tear one page at a time, tossing them into the water. Cleopatra enters.)

CLEOPATRA: Stop.

ANAÏS: The history of my life. Gone.

CLEOPATRA: No.

ANAÏS: It's a liberation! A freedom!

CLEOPATRA: This is the symbol of you.

ANAÏS: They called me a feminist! Why? A feminist because I wrote the word penis!

CLEOPATRA: You freed women from being ashamed that we enjoyed men.

ANAÏS: Yes! Without enjoying ourselves.

CLEOPATRA: I'm sure you enjoyed yourself.

ANAÏS: I did… Yes. But all I gave to women were stories about men.

CLEOPATRA: I would have thought you would want to keep them.

ANAÏS: The only reason to look to the past is to see how you've changed. How can you sit here—reliving memories of yourself? Were you so great that time should stop for you?

CLEOPATRA: No.

ANAÏS: Then stay and create something new. If we are not nothing—if we continue, then continue with me.

CLEOPATRA: Finding my child is the root of who I am.

ANAÏS: I do not want to be alone.

CLEOPATRA: I thought of all the women, you would desire to leave the most. To grow—to change—to move.

ANAÏS: I was never satisfied. If I cannot simply be peaceful with myself…who I was—who I am—then I cannot enjoy this world.

CLEOPATRA: I must find my child.

ANAÏS: I want to be with you; someone I like and have fun with. Fuck discovery. Do not go with this man. It will kill everything I've done since I got here.

(Beat.)

CLEOPATRA: I must find my son.

ANAÏS: I know where they all are. Victoria's Albert, Joan's Jesus, Andromeda's Perseus, my father, Heloise's Abelard—

CLEOPATRA: Tell me where I may find my son.

ANAÏS: Your son is with his father on the Island of Great Men.

CLEOPATRA: Where are they?

ANAÏS: So close—to the east. You can't see because of the fog, but it's there. It isn't what you think. I said, "Take me to the island where the greatest men, the great rulers and thinkers can be found." And I was there. Imagine an island with Julius Caesar, Napoleon, Malcolm X, Franklin Roosevelt, Henry the Fifth, Oscar Wilde, and Jesus all live sort of. Do you know what they do? Do you? They fight. I arrived–searching for someone. I was searching for Henry Miller–my man, thinker, and wisdom. He was there. Bombs were going off in every direction. Caesar had almost conquered the entire land, but Marc Antony betrayed him to the Americans. I arrived and not a single man looked at me. The smoke from their wars has created a curtain of ash around the entire island, and they haven't even noticed. They have walled themselves in a furnace with a fire that can never be extinguished until all of the men have been consumed by it. I stripped naked and walked between trenches and tanks, boats and barges full of angry, bleeding men. And they didn't look at me. I saw your son, a beautiful young boy at the side of Julius Caesar who was instructing him in the art of war. Finally, I found my Henry in the midst of it. He was sitting on the ground, writing. I spoke to him. He smiled and said he was busy, but we could have sex later if I was still in the mood. It was as if he hadn't thought of me in years. While the thought of him had been in my mind every second. A day did not go by without me secretly chanting his name. They only have one thought; to conquer–to be superior–to rule. So I walked back to the boat and begged to be taken where I would never be followed by those men. Take me to an island where these men would never come. I am not saying that your experience would be the same. They'll notice you if you play by their rules. If you battle as they do–which is what you did in life. You played by their rules to advance. Will you do that now?

CLEOPATRA: Why would you deny me, or the others the right to choose?

ANAÏS: I had gone through that experience for all of us.

CLEOPATRA: My child.

ANAÏS: You're dead—he's dead—move on.

CLEOPATRA: Nothing gives you the right to destroy someone's world.

ANAÏS: Truth gives you the right to tear down gods if they are false.

CLEOPATRA: You cannot grow anymore. In life— you'd finished your journey—and you want to change us to feel that you have a purpose still. My purpose was to wait—to be reunited with my son. To raise a man to know that power does not come from winning or knowing… it comes from being.

ANAÏS: Be with me. Be my friend.

CLEOPATRA: You are like us. Stuck in the journey of your life. The ferryman brought you exactly where you belong.

(Anaïs exits. Cleopatra is alone for a moment. She violently pushes all of the books in the water. When she touches the water, she makes a wish—almost instinctively. After an ominous beat, a man rises from the water and into her arms. It is Marc Antony. He kisses her deeply and slides on top of her. After an intense bit of grinding, he belts out a hearty laugh, rolls off of her. Both sit side by side on the shore.)

ANTONY: You called?

CLEOPATRA *(warmly)*: Antony.

ANTONY: It's been a long time so the first one is going to be quick but just give me a few minutes and we'll do it again.

CLEOPATRA *(a big laugh)*: I've missed you.

ANTONY: I'm not kidding, it's been a long time…

(Cleopatra slaps him. Antony slaps her back.)

CLEOPATRA: You can go now.

ANTONY: I waited on an island shore a hundred years for you.

CLEOPATRA: Did you? Did you wait?

ANTONY: Of course.

CLEOPATRA: Pathetic.

ANTONY: Bitch.

CLEOPATRA *(rising)*: You are dismissed.

ANTONY: You called me.

(Antony grabs her and throws her to the ground he leaps on her. The two squirm together—each fighting to be on top. They roll around for a moment before both give up and separate.)

ANTONY: Was it ever written that we were failed lovers?

CLEOPATRA: No.

ANTONY: We were.

CLEOPATRA: Yes.

ANTONY: Not for lack of trying.

CLEOPATRA: No.

ANTONY: And we came close that one time.

CLEOPATRA: Yes.

ANTONY: I always thought it'd get better but it never did.

CLEOPATRA: No.

ANTONY: When I masturbate to the idea of you it's always more satisfying.

CLEOPATRA: You always bite me and you sometimes smell.

ANTONY: Sex had to be on your terms.

CLEOPATRA: Only because you were bad at it.

(They smile and kiss, friends.)

ANTONY: Are you alone here?

CLEOPATRA: No. There are women.

ANTONY: Can I watch?

CLEOPATRA: After two thousand years of representing female strength I have grown tired of women. And I grew tired of men while still alive.

ANTONY: You'll never tire. You are strength eternal.

(They kiss.)

CLEOPATRA: Bring me my child.

(Beat.)

ANTONY: Yes.

CLEOPATRA: Yes.

ANTONY: Call him. I thought you called me. I thought forever you would call me.

CLEOPATRA: Bring him to me.

ANTONY: I thought you would want to make love. I thought you would want to fight once more. But you call and ask me to bring you another man's child. I have come for you. I have waited for you. I have hurt for you. I have wanted to hurt you—because we both enjoyed hurting so much.

CLEOPATRA: Bring him to me.

ANTONY: He is not yours anymore.

CLEOPATRA: Antony.

ANTONY: Choose me.

(Beat.)

CLEOPATRA: I died with you once already my friend.

ANTONY: Why would you stay here? I will take you to him. Be with us both. So you don't want to be a lover anymore—or a fighter. I get that. It's natural. It is time for you to be a mother. Play at that for a thousand years if you like—but do it with me.

CLEOPATRA: And if I did neither? What would I be?

ANTONY: I built a statue of gold in your image that is worshipped by thousands. I will lay at your feet as a dog to kick and rule. I will rub oils on your skin— taste you and love you however you like. I will caress your thighs and worship your womb as a humble slave. Be with me. I have waited.

CLEOPATRA: I have learned about people who wait. It is empty.

(Antony looks at her for one final time, and goes back into the water. Cleopatra looks after him. Andromeda enters hurriedly. She looks at Cleopatra.)

ANDROMEDA: Was there a man here?

CLEOPATRA: Not really.

ANDROMEDA: Cleo, are you helping with the raft?

CLEOPATRA: No.

ANDROMEDA: Can I tell you something? Something very personal?

CLEOPATRA: No.

ANDROMEDA: I'm not either. And I am shocked at myself—but every time I begin, I get distracted... And...I feel alive!

CLEOPATRA: So do I.

ANDROMEDA: I haven't even looked at that water! Not in the longest time... Remember when we were on this island—alone? Just the two of us? *(Cleopatra stops smiling.)* I kept our secret. I never told anyone how many times you tried to kill yourself. Every time I'd speak you'd start looking for another snake. That's not who you are anymore.

BLACKOUT

SCENE 3:

(Same as before. Now, A raft built of the skeletal white Birches sits on the bank. Bosie and Victoria are alone, admiring their handiwork.)

VICTORIA: A fine craft! A superior vessel of transport to my Albert.

BOSIE: One would think it was built by professionals, rather than a Lord and Lady of leisure.

VICTORIA: That is the difference between educated and uneducated people. Uneducated people do manual labor and think that educated people are incapable of doing it. Educated people know that they *are* capable of doing it, but choose not to.

BOSIE: It's true, they are not burdened with knowledge.

VICTORIA: I love this knot you tied at the starboard bow.

BOSIE: Thank you, your majesty.

VICTORIA: Wherever did you learn how to do that?

BOSIE: From a fisherman I fornicated with in Venice.

VICTORIA: Tell me Lord Alfred, were you faithful to Oscar Wilde?

BOSIE: Were you faithful to Albert?

VICTORIA: Of course I was.

BOSIE: And of course I wasn't.

VICTORIA: You poofters aren't the faithful kind.

BOSIE: I don't believe we've been given the chance.

VICTORIA: You know that is the problem I always had with homosexuals. They remind me that men see sexual intercourse as pleasurable regardless of whom they're with.

BOSIE: I believe we've fewer differences than you imagine. *(Beat)* Will this raft hold all of us?

VICTORIA: If it doesn't, then we'll just toss someone overboard.

(Victoria picks up the conch shell and blows. The women enter: Cleopatra with Anaïs and Heloise with Andromeda.)

VICTORIA: The ship is ready.

BOSIE: There's no time to waste!

ANAÏS: There is no time.

BOSIE: How did you die? Did someone kill you? I am sure someone must have killed you.

ANAÏS: I am not going.

CLEOPATRA: I am staying as well.

ANDROMEDA: You are?

CLEOPATRA: If I need a man all I have to do is call him.

BOSIE: Too bad. If the Hydra came after us, I was going to throw you over as a distraction.

VICTORIA: I hear by declare Bosie Douglas my right-hand man. From here on out I declare that it shall be forgotten that he is a homosexual.

HELOISE: I am staying as well.

ANAÏS: That is good.

HELOISE: I'll probably regret the decision later.

ANAÏS: It's the right decision for the person you are now.

BOSIE: So that leaves three of us?

VICTORIA: Come Andromeda.

(Andromeda steps forward. Heloise grabs her and pulls her aside. The others watch.)

HELOISE: You are staying.

ANDROMEDA: I have to find my Perseus.

HELOISE: But you said you were staying.

ANDROMEDA: I never did.

HELOISE: Andromeda.

ANDROMEDA: Come with us, Heloise. You are my protector.

HELOISE: Stay with me.

ANDROMEDA: I have to find my Perseus. That is who I am.

HELOISE: You aren't an accent to someone else's reality.

(Beat.)

ANDROMEDA: Will we still be friends? Are you disappointed in me?

HELOISE: Yes.

ANDROMEDA: You're disappointed in me?

HELOISE: Yes.

ANDROMEDA: No… You are hurting me.

HELOISE: Stay with me. I love you. All the parts of you.

ANDROMEDA: And I love you.

(Andromeda crosses to the boat.)

VICTORIA: Wait! One more!

(Bosie walks upstage and picks up the sleeping Joan and brings her to the raft.)

BOSIE: Who's he?

VICTORIA: She's my Joan of Arc. I think she's like you in a way. *(Beat.)* Which direction?

ANAÏS: There. *(She points them in the direction of the men. Beat.)* Your Albert's always known where you are. He chose not to come.

(A long beat.)

VICTORIA: I hereby release my claim on this island and rename it, Anaïs Nin: The Island of the Useless.

ANAÏS: Au revoir.

VICTORIA: Farewell.

(Karen Carpenter walks onto her island.)

KAREN *(sung)*: We've only just begun to live.
    Screw all their promises.
    Without them we're on our way.

BOSIE: What is this?

VICTORIA: Karen Carpenter is sending us off!

BOSIE: I love her voice!

(Bosie dances as the raft floats off stage.)

ANAÏS *(to Karen)*: This is better.

KAREN *(sung)*: And yes, we've just begun

(Anaïs blows her a kiss. Karen exits.)

HELOISE: She's leaving now...She's gone... Do you think she'll remember me? She forgets. She forgets things.

ANAÏS: You are very brave.

HELOISE: I knew Andromeda for centuries. Longer than I ever knew Abelard. I loved her more all along and she was sitting right next to me.

CLEOPATRA: So, what do you think we should do?

ANAÏS: I don't know.

HELOISE: What do you mean?

(The women stare at each other.)

ANAÏS: Well...first, we have to let go of who we were. All those battles are done. *(Anaïs lets down her hair.)* We were brave and changed thinking. Yes. But we must also change now. Not freeze in it. *(Anaïs takes off any jewelry she is wearing.)* We strip ourselves of everything and stand naked as a new woman. A woman past the fight for a voice. A woman who has found her voice and allows it to be heard. Simply and beautifully. *(Anaïs takes off her stockings.)* We accept each other wholly and enjoy the presence of our womanhood!

HELOISE: Anaïs. Sweetheart. Keep your clothes on please.

(Beat. Anaïs stops, stunned.)

HELOISE: I don't need to see you naked to know who you are. I got it.

(Cleopatra is beside herself.)

ANAÏS: I will just take off my blouse.

HELOISE: No! No.

(Anaïs looks at Cleopatra.)

CLEOPATRA: No.

ANAÏS: You inhibit me.

HELOISE: Awww. Sweetheart.

ANAÏS: You are disagreeable women.

(Heloise looks at Cleopatra and both start laughing un-controllably. They go to Anaïs and hug her. After a beat of this, Heloise puts her head in Anaïs' lap.)

HELOISE: Anaïs…tell me a story.

ANAÏS: I don't want us to talk about men. But I want you to start the story for me…

(Neither knows what to say. Then, a new woman walks onstage. It is Frida Khalo with flowers surrounding her face.)

CLEOPATRA: Hello?

FRIDA: Hemos oído de ustedes! Este lugar! Bello! Soy Frida. *(Beat)* There are more of us!

ANAÏS: Yes!

BLACKOUT.

END OF PLAY

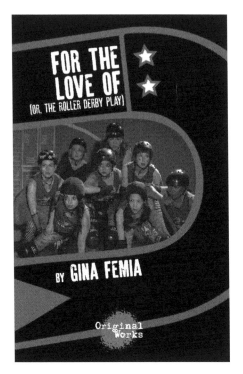

<u>**FOR THE LOVE OF**</u>
<u>(or, the roller derby play)</u>
By Gina Femia

Synopsis: When Joy gets on the Brooklyn Scallywags and meets the star, Lizzie Lightning, she and her long term partner Michelle find their lives turned upside down. *For The Love Of* asks how much you're willing to sacrifice – or lose – in order to follow your heart.

Cast Size: 9 Diverse Females

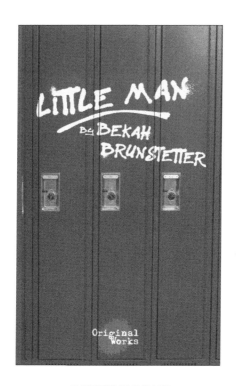

LITTLE MAN
by Bekah Brunstetter

Synopsis: Howie has spent the last decade trying to forget the traumas of high school. But when an invitation to his ten year reunion arrives, he hops on a plane home to discover just what happened to the jocks, the prom queens, and the social outcasts- and whether anyone cares that he's a millionaire now. With wry wit and penetrating insight, Bekah Brunstetter's heartbreaking comedy takes us on a hilariously awkward and unexpectedly moving journey in which no one can completely abandon who they used to be.

Cast Size: 3 Males, 3 Females

NOTES

NOTES

NOTES